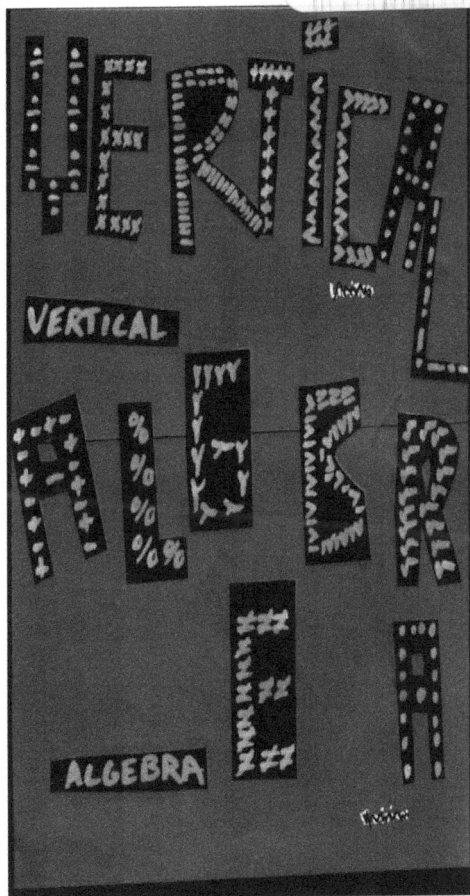

**Inspirational Success Quotationeth
De Black Englishmeneth Sir
Kedcuv Rhinclavu IV**

**Translationeth: Mansu Edwards
and Crater Rock Alien
From South East Mars**

Ye Words De English Inspirational: "Downloadeth God's wordeth for prosperity andeth peace." - Sir Kedcuv Rhinclavu IV

21st Century Translation: "Download God's word for prosperity and peace." – Mansu Edwards

South East Mars Galaxy Translation: Donaxala God's h:w<^> vyfri poscavuim >>? ++^ - Crater Rock Alien

Ye Words De English Inspirational: "Rusheth to your dreameth instead of a jobeth."- Sir Kedcuv Rhinclavu IV

21st Century Translation: "Rush to your dreams instead of a 9-5." - Mansu Edwards

South East Mars Galaxy Translation: Beqfacivo xaz viyamot dreoca insafaseyl fegrevinchui qes# 5-9vedved – Crater Rock Alien

Ye Words De English Inspirational: "Thee registrationeth period foreth success is always open." - Sir Kedcuv Rhinclavu IV

21st Century Translation: "The registration period for success is always open." – Mansu Edwards

South East Mars Galaxy Translation: "Rsashas keeceebee lacucu vyfri batwaba tiwax va6a spavivi8." – Crater Rock Alien

Ye Words De English Inspirational: "I don't needeth a second opinioneth on myeth dreams." – Sir Kedcuv Rhinclavu

21st Century Translation: "I don't need a second opinion on my dreams" – Mansu Edwards

South East Mars Galaxy Translation: "9^ h@balax javussapot qes# sexdyasa obegjaja rycwehs *c< dreoca – Crater Rock Alien

Ye Words De English Inspirational: "My life isn't perfecteth but, I'll die improvingeth it." – Sir Kedcuv Rhinclavu IV

21st Century Translation: "My life isn't perfect, but I'll die improving it." – Mansu Edwards

South East Mars Galaxy Translation: *c< rupubabu uyewqa pacataseybu, buebuebue Ivabese d=patpat evgazhimibidisheopop vxvxn – Crater Rock Alien

Ye Words De English Inspirational: "Most peopleth get an A+ in talking and an F in doingeth." - Sir Kedcuv Rhinclavu IV

21st Century Translation: "Most people get a A+ in talking and a F in doing." – Mansu Edwards

South East Mars Galaxy Translation: Rerackx puvweqqq bibo0x qes# Laqtuu brutiffi u >>? qes# cwenck @^ zyleafi – Crater Rock Alien

Ye Words De English Inspirational: "Worry gives your success tendinitis." – Sir Kedcuv Rhinclavu IV

21st Century Translation: "Worry gives your success tendinitis." – Mansu Edwards

South East Mars Galaxy Translation: "Gavacabapoewew Heclowz gexa yzfui8 tendionickz" – Crater Rock Alien

Alien Galaxy Boot Pronunciation Index

@^

Eye – Cuh

batwaba

Ba – Twah – Ba

beqfacivo

Beck – Fah – See – Vo

bibo0x

Bi – Bow – Zeer – Oh – Sa

brutiffi

Brew – Tiff – E

buebuebue

Buay – Buay - Buay

*c<

Star – Cee – Less

cwenck

Kwunk

d=patpat

Dee – Pa – Pa

Donaxala

Dah – Nocks – A – La

dreoca

Dray – Oh – Kah

evgazhimibidisheopop

Eve – Gas – Him – A –
Beed – I – Key – Ob

fegrevinchui

Feej – Reev – In – Kui

Gavacabapoewew

Gav – Ah – Sha – Bas –
Ah – Pa – Pa

Gexa

Hay - Ga

h@balax

H – At – Buh – Locks

h:w<^>

Hay – Wee

Heclowz

Hee – Clow – Zee

insafaseyl

In – Safe – Assail

Ivabese

I've – Uh – Bee – Say

javussapot

Jay – Vuz – A – Po

keeceebee

Kitch – Ceechee - Bee

lacucu

Lah – Koop – Koo

Laqtuu

Lock – Two

obegjaja

Oh – Bah – Juh – Hey

pacataseybu

Pack – Aye – Tah – Say – Boo

poscavium

Poscavium

puvweqqq

Poov – Way – Eck – Eck –
Eck

qes#

Kay

Rerackx

Ree – Ray – Ox

Rsashas

Are – Sash – Us

rupubabu

Roo – Poo – Bah – Bu

rycwehs

Rice – Ways

sexdyasa

Says – Die – Ah - Sah

Spavivi8

Spa – Vy – Vee –
Eightchi

tendionickz

Tendionickz

tiwax

Tie – Wacks

u>>?

Ooh – Tray – Kay - Nah

Uyewqa

Yuca

va6a

Vay - Sir

viyamot

Vigh – A – Mut

vxvxn

Vex – Uh – Noon

vyfri

Vigh – Eh - Free

xaz

Say – Chuh

yzfui8

Ease – Freight

zyleafi

Zigh – Leaf – E

>>?

Gas – Ma – Vay – Aye –
Ock

++^

Pizz – Ye – Coo – Voo –
Boo

9^

Yah – Cax – Cuee – See –
Dew – Bacha

5-9vedved

Woo – Loo – High – Gee – Gee

Contact Info

concreteposture@gmail.com

https://www.facebook.com/mansu.e dwards

www.twitter.com/Ohassa

pierre

la fluent's

dictionary

A
MANSU
EDWARDS
PRODUCTION

Creative handwriting: Sloppy, messy penmanship.

Aggressive breath: Bad breath.

Lavish breath: Pleasant, beautiful or exotic breath.

Inverted odor: A bad odor.

Conferencing: Gossiping.

Cornerstore Dwella: A person who stands outside a cornerstore everyday.

A.N.A. (Ask-N-Answer): A woman simultaneously asking and answering a question.

Radiate: To get angry.

Feudal Town: A residential area.

Concrete Hallways: The streets.

Hall Monitors: The Police.

Hall Pass: Driver's License, Passport, or any form of Government ID.

Incubating: Thinking.

Pre-heating: Gathering courage.

Assistant Principal: The Mayor.

Principal: The United States President.

Audition: A guy introducing himself or talking to random girls in the streets.

Empty calories: A brief meeting between a man or woman that doesn't go anywhere ie. relationship, dating, friendship.

Bowels growling: Having gas.

Season Finale: New Year's Eve.

Season Premiere: New Year's Day.

Time Out Corner: Jail.

Lam: Lamborghini.

Homeroom: Home.

Top Soil: Aristocracy.

Nipple: A pimple

Barracks: Apartment.

Brown Petroleum: Iced Tea.

Mason Dixon Line: Hairline.

Aviating: Exaggerating.

Emperor: A landlord.

Neapolitan: A male/female mixed with 3 or more races.

Intellectual Property: The Mind.

World Premiere: 1st meeting between two people.

Pollinating: Thinking.

Mental Renovation: Clearing the mind.

Food Racist: A person who discriminates against ethnic foods.

Stuttering: Repeating mistakes.

Blocked pores: Narrowmindedness.

Lockerroom: Underwear.

Plains: Body hair.

Blocked pores:
Narrowminded.

Exit Interview: Death.

Commercial Break: A nap.

Trial Period: When a man and woman are engaged to be married.

Vegetation: Facial hair.

Windows: Glasses.

Sequencing: Combining ideas.

Daycare Center: Bra

Tune off: Go to sleep.

Shot clock: Traffic light.

Niagara Falls: Champagne

Sentences

1. John's creative handwriting caught the eyes of his classmate, Bob.

2. Her aggressive breath instantaneously subdued the wild pitbull.

3. Her lavish breath smelled like a mixture of chamomile and citrus fruit.

4. The woman's inverted odor was encased in a capsule for scientific experimentation.

5. Joel was conferencing with his friends on the platform until the train arrived.

6. During the afternoons, Jay and the Cornerstore Dwella play cribbage at the Chicken Spot.

7. A.N.A. asked her
    boyfriend questions in
    Russian and answered in
    Japanese.

8. The radiation inhibited
    his thinking and
    breathing

9. Ramone and his boys went clubbing to the Feudal town on Fridays because of the unfathomable ration of women to men.

10.   Pablo and Dietrick gave
each other icy
looks as they walked
passed each other in the
concrete hallways.

11. The community were suspicious of hall monitors because of the recent skirmishes in the project buildings.

12. Joan had to revew her hall pass at the D.M.V.

13. The pigeon chirped at him while he was incubating on the park bench.

14. As the speaker spoke, Lewis mumbled biblical hymns to initiate the preheating process for a successful speech.

15. The Assistant Principal's televised speech is critiqued at the top 50 law schools in America.

16. The Principal blogs
    under anonymity for
    security purposes.

17. Clevon auditions 20
    times a day to improve his
    communication skills and
    confidence.

18. After, the woman left the bar, Harold yelled 'that's only empty calories', I can get more.

19. The undercooked meat from the restaurant made his bowels growl.

20. The Season Finale brought people from across the world to Times Square.

21. The Season Premier made many people reflect on the past year.

22. The criminals studied self-help principles in the Time Out Corner.

23. The 3030 Lam had seven seats and a hybrid jet chopper engine.

24. Rodney gave the babysitter a bonus for staying an extra two hours in homeroom to take care of his 4-month-old son.

25.   The top soil taught
      Financial Education
      courses to the low income
      tenants.

26. Shelly has an elongated
    nipple above her left elbow.

27. Naimah cleaned the
    barracks after the guest
    party.

28. The secret ingredient to Hanson's Brown Petroleum is processed lychee.

29. Merrick's Mason Dixon line is captured on the 2016 All Star Barber poster.

30. Melina aviated her encounter with her boyfriend at the Disco showcase.

31. The Emperor emailed new rent leases to pre-existing tenants.

32. The Neapolitan teenager regrets learning that his ancestors were Ku Klux Klan members.

33. Matthew's intellectual
     property is filled with wealth
     and happiness.

34. The World premier
     morphed into dating and
     then marriage.

35. Liberia always pollinates in her office after lunch.

36. Scientist's affirmed that an individual's mental renovation accelerates in a peaceful environment.

37. The Food Racist spoke
     for 45 minutes on Broccoli's
     superiority to Eggplant.

38. Vina's stuttering
     confused family and
     friends.

39.　Peter's blocked pores infuriated his business partners.

40.　After Kitoubo's exit interview he flew into Christ's arms.

41. Hykim took a commercial
     break during the Scuba
     Diving National Anthem.

42. The trial period between
     Markis and Althena began
     in Morocco.

43.   His vegetation needed trimming every week at Jack's Salon.

44.   Her windows were admired by the Fashionista bloggers.

45. The sequencing between James and Milrana made them 100 million dollars in 10 days.

46.   Her daycare center glowed under her white buttoned shirt.

47.   Pablo recorded Alonzo tuning off during a lap dance at a Strip Club.

48.   The Queen Size bed exercise between the couple resulted in her man having a pelvic cramp.

49.   Sherita was feeling on Jose's circumcision on the Stock Market trading floor.

50. The shot clock malfunctioned each day at 4:00pm during rush hour.

51. The Niagara Falls dripped from his joyous lips.

Peace 2 God